Look Out for Animals

CONTENTS

NATIONAL GEOGRAPHIC School Publishing
Hampton-Brown

Final Blends

Look at each picture. Read the words.

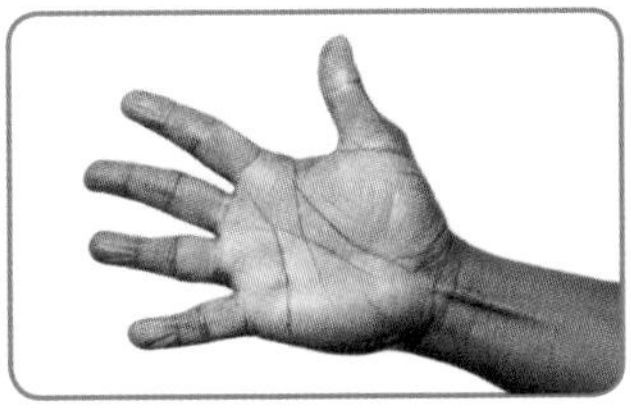

ha**nd**

sa**nd**

ve**st**

la**mp**

sta**mp**

a**nt**

High Frequency Words

- could
- good
- hard
- now
- over
- part
- under
- very

Key Words

Look at the picture. Read the clues.
Can you and a partner find a bug?

Where Is It?

1. It is **very hard** to find.
2. **Now** it looks like **part** of a stick.
3. It **could** be **under** or **over** a leaf.
4. This can be a very **good** trick!
5. Can you see it now?

Phonics Games
NGReach.com

The Best Trick

by Kate Pershing

Inspect this plant. What could hide here?

Here is a hint. It is hard to see. It can blend in and hide. It looks like the plant. It is a bug! This is a very good trick!

Now inspect these sticks. The sticks are bent. The sticks have bumps. Look at the end of the stick. What can you find?

What animal is that? This is a hint. Its body looks like part of a stick. It is a stick bug.

Inspect these rocks. They are very hard and wet. You could slip on them. But you could trip on an animal, too.

What is it? Here is a hint! It looks just like a rock. If you could just bend over to look, you could see it. It is a plump little crab! Did it trick you?

Inspect this place. There is an animal that spends its days in the hot sun here. It can hide in the dust and sand. It can hide under a rock. What could it be?

This is a hint. It blends into the rock. But if you see it, jump back fast! It is a big snake!

Inspect the grass. A big animal can blend in. It can seem lost in the grass. What animal do you think it could be?

A lion can hide in this grass. Is this the best trick of all? If not, pick the one that is best to you.

Now inspect these animals. What hiding tricks do you think they have?

Final Blends

Read these words.

spend	bend	fast	flop
dust	blend	hunt	stand

Find the words with final blends.
Use letters to build them.

s t a n d

Talk Together

Look at the picture. Use words from the box above to tell a partner about what a lion can do.

A lion can stand.

Syllable Division

Look at each picture. Read the words.

Example:

antler

pumpkin

hundred

children

mattress

gumdrop

High Frequency Words
could
good
hard
now
over
part
under
very

Key Words

Read the sentences. Match each sentence to one of the pictures.

Tundra Animals

1. This one is **hard** to see **now**.
2. This one runs fast **over** the grass.
3. This one is **under part** of a plant.
4. This one has a **very good** set of antlers.
5. **Could** you see them?

Which animal was very hard to see?

Phonics Games

NGReach.com

A Trip to the Tundra

by Kathryn Mead

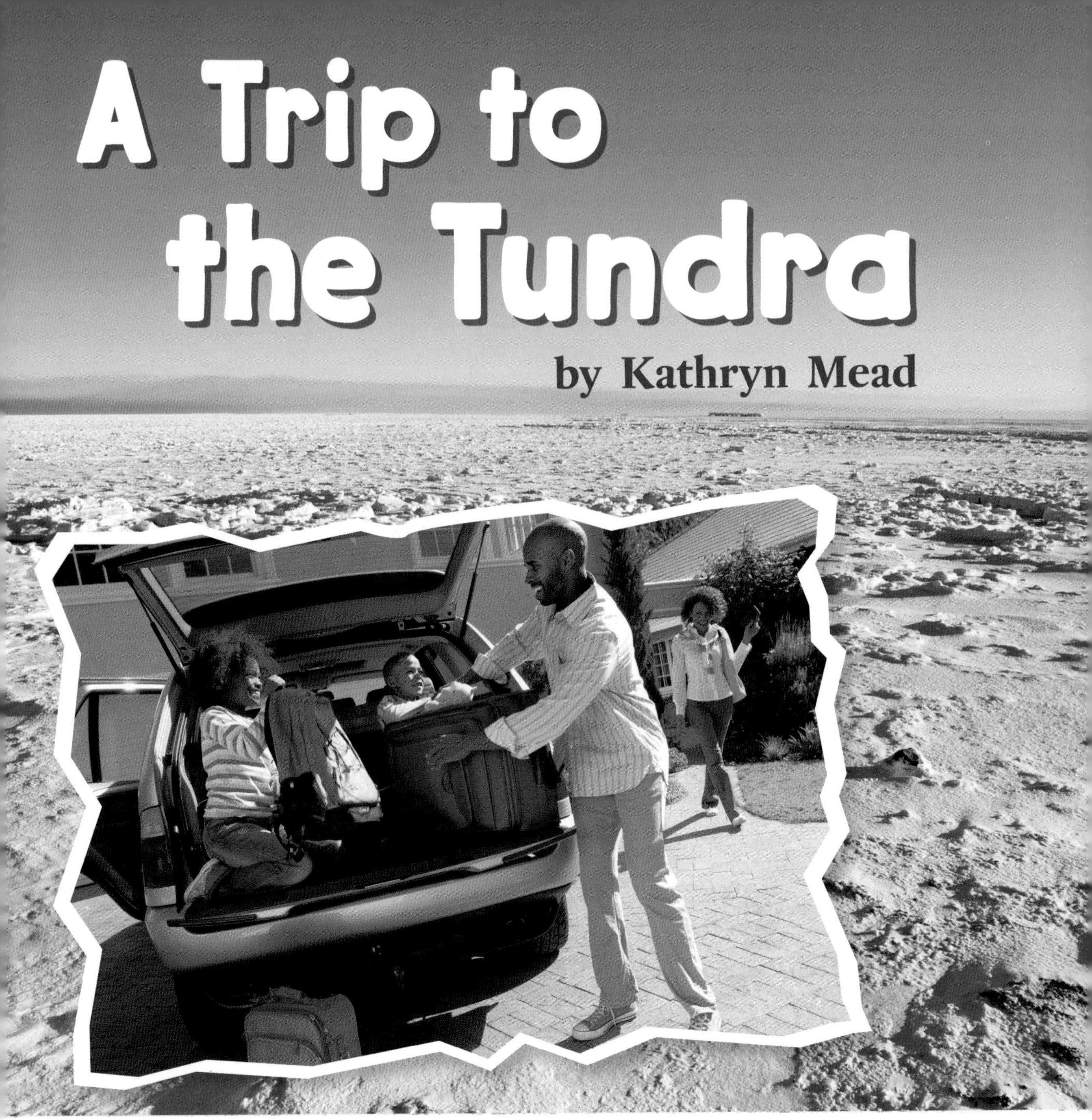

Do you like to go on trips? We could go on a trip to the tundra. You could contrast it to your home.

We must hop on a jet. Pack a very good map. Bring thick socks!

The tundra is very flat and white.

If you like frost and snow, you will like the tundra.

The tundra attracts a lot of animals. We will see how they can make a good home in the tundra.

We see hundreds of animals there. Look at this pale fox. See how its pale fur helps it hide?

An arctic hare runs past us. There are hundreds of them on the tundra. We see it for an instant as it skids over the hard snow.

We see this huge animal. It has a thick blanket of fur and a rack of big antlers.

People come to the tundra now to see the polar bear. You must not come in contact with this bear!

If you could inspect a polar bear, you could find thick fat under its skin. This thick fat helps the polar bear be warm.

Now we have to go home. What was the very best part of the trip? Are you glad you went?

Syllable Division

Read these words.

instant	pumpkin	inspect	contrast
antlers	hundred	mattress	children

Find words with 2 syllables. Use letters to build them.

i n s t a n t

Talk Together

You can take trips to lots of places—a store, a farm, a zoo. Look at these pictures. Use the words from the box above to tell your partner what you look at.

I inspect the pumpkin.

Help Little Crab Get Home

Take turns with a partner. Use game markers. Read the words, and then move your markers.

END
children
instant
constant
clump
part
pump
plant
contrast
inspect
under

Acknowledgments
Grateful acknowledgment is given to the authors, artists, photographers, museums, publishers, and agents for permission to reprint copyrighted material. Every effort has been made to secure the appropriate permission. If any omissions have been made or if corrections are required, please contact the Publisher.

Photographic Credits
CVR (b) Blacqbook/Shutterstock. (bg) Borut Trdina/iStockphoto. (tl) B.G. Smith/Shutterstock. (tr) Stephen Inglis/Shutterstock. **2** (bl) Mark Thiessen/Hampton-Brown/National Geographic School Publishing. (br) orionmystery@flickr/Shutterstock. (cl) Jitalia17/iStockphoto. (cr) Kenneth C. Zirkel/iStockphoto. (tl) Peter Nguyen/iStockphoto. (tr) Robert Glusic/PhotoDisc/Getty Images. **3** (b) Liz Garza Williams/Hampton-Brown/National Geographic School Publishing. (t) Thomas Marent/Minden Pictures. **4** (b) Artville. **4-5** (bg) David Chia/Alamy Images. **5** (r) Ch'ien C. Lee/Photographer's Direct. **6-7** (bg) Tim Laman/National Geographic Image Collection. **7** (r) Joel Sartore/National Geographic Image Collection. **8-9** (bg) Amy Riley/iStockphoto. **9** (r) Piotr Naskrecki/Minden Pictures. **10-11** (bg) Sam Abell/National Geographic Image Collection. **11** (r) Corel. **12-13** (bg) EcoPrint/Shutterstock. **13** (r) EcoPrint/Shutterstock. **14** (bg) Patrick Robbins/iStockphoto. (bl) Raymonf Gehman/National Geographic Image Collection. (r) John Foxx Images/Imagestate. (tl) Max Voran/National Geographic Image Collection. **15** Liz Garza Williams/Hampton-Brown/National Geographic School Publishing. **16** (bl) Mats/Shutterstock. (br) GWImages/Shutterstock. (cr) BananaStock/Jupiterimages. (tl) Dawn Nichols/iStockphoto. (tr) David T. Gomez/iStockphoto. **17** (br) Liz Garza Williams/Hampton-Brown/National Geographic School Publishing. (cl) Corel. (cr) Konrad Wothe/Minden Pictures/National Geographic Image Collection. (tl) John Pitcher/iStockphoto. (tr) James Gritz/age fotostock. **18** (bg) Nicolas Chan/Alamy Images. (inset) Juice Images/age fotostock. **19** (bg) Dave Gitlin/iStockphoto. (bl) Slobo Mitic/iStockphoto. (br) Burke/Triolo/Jupiterimages. (t) Andrey Yurlov/Shutterstock. **20-21** (bg) Dave Gitlin/iStockphoto. (inset) Roger Leo/Index Stock/age fotostock. **22-23** (bg) Dave Gitlin/iStockphoto. (inset) David Parsons/iStockphoto. **24** (inset) Tom Mangelsen/Nature Picture Library. **24-25** (bg) Dave Gitlin/iStockphoto. **25** (inset) Asgeir Helgestad/Nature Picture Library. **26-27** (bg) Dave Gitlin/iStockphoto. (inset) Mitsuaki Iwago/Minden Pictures/National Geographic Image Collection. **28** (bg) Dave Gitlin/iStockphoto. (inset) Ilja Masík/Shutterstock. **29** Liz Garza Williams/Hampton-Brown/National Geographic School Publishing.

Illustrator Credits
15, **29** Mircea Catusanu; **30-31** Mattia Cerato

National Geographic School Publishing
Hampton-Brown
www.NGSP.com

Printed in the USA.
Quad Graphics, Leominster, MA

ISBN:978-0-7362-8061-7

17 18 19
10 9 8 7 6